The Good Fun! Book

12 Months of Parties That Celebrate Service

by Karen Duncan & Kate Hannigan Issa

Illustrated by Anthony Alex LeTourneau

Published by Blue Marlin Publications

Text copyright © 2010 by Karen Duncan and Kate Hannigan Issa
Illustrations copyright © 2010 by Anthony Alex LeTourneau
Book design & layout by Anthony Alex LeTourneau

First printing 2010
Job # 126396
Printed and bound by Friesens Book Division in Altona, Manitoba, Canada

Library of Congress Cataloging-in-Publication Data

Duncan, Karen, 1970-
 The good fun! book : 12 months of parties that celebrate service / by
Karen Duncan and Kate Hannigan Issa. -- 1st ed.
     p. cm.
 Includes bibliographical references and index.
 ISBN-13: 978-0-9792918-5-2 (hardcover : alk. paper)
 ISBN-10: 0-9792918-5-2 (hardcover : alk. paper) 1. Parties. 2.
Handicraft. 3. Cookery. I. Issa, Kate Hannigan, 1967- II. Title.
TX731.D794 2010
642'.4--dc22
                    2010025848

Blue Marlin Publications, Ltd.
823 Aberdeen Road, West Bay Shore, NY 11706
www.bluemarlinpubs.com

For Arne, Claire and Ryan, who love good fun! — KD

For my party people, Olivia, Nolan and Gabriel. And of course, Norm. — KHI

For Sophie. Celebrate the fun in every day. — AAL

What do adults do when they want to help out their favorite charity? Often they throw a big gala, get dressed up in fancy clothes, and invite all their friends. They have a great time spreading the word about the organization while raising money at the same time.

Why should you have to wait until you're grown up to get in on the action?

You can have a fun time for a good cause every month of the year! All you need to do is look around at the people and places that might need a little help in your neighborhood, and get started! Throw a party with a purpose and invite all your friends to come. Or talk to your teacher and host one in your classroom.

Some of the parties we suggest will work better at school, where you can tap into the power of your peers. Other parties work better at home, where you can invite special friends over to focus on an issue that's close to your heart — whether it's helping animals, feeding the hungry, or cheering up seniors. We hope you'll pick out your favorite activities and create original parties of your own!

Every month presented here is different, but they share the same five features:

2 activities to help your community
1 delicious treat to make and serve at your party
1 take-home activity for you and your friends to enjoy
1 charity to get to know

It all adds up to good fun. And, unlike your parents, you don't have to wear a ball gown or a tuxedo to make a difference!

JANUARY

Please come to...
AN ANIMAL-LOVERS PARTY!

What to bring:
Cat or dog toy
Cat or dog collar
Dog leash
Old pillowcase

WHAT YOU CAN DO:

You'll see plenty of tail-wagging excitement at an animal-themed party. Celebrate all kinds of critters by putting up paw-print decorations and serving snacks that have an animal theme. Plan your activities around helping local animals in shelters within your community. But don't stop there: you can help animals around the world by supporting groups that work on behalf of animal issues. Here's a quick list of party ideas:

1. **Make dog and cat goodie bags.**
2. **Make dog beds out of old pillowcases.**
3. **Decorate cat-cakes for you and your friends to eat.**
4. **Bake dog biscuits to take home and share with dogs in your life.**
5. **Learn about Operation Migration, which helps endangered whooping cranes.**

HAVE A HOWLING GOOD TIME!

Everyone loves animals, whether they're furry, feathered or even the scaly kind. But did you know that stray or abandoned animals fill shelters in cities across the country? While they wait for a friendly family to adopt them, shelter dogs and cats will need all the tender loving care they can get. Consider making their lives a little brighter by donating pet supplies and toys to a shelter, and even making them a comfy bed.

MAKING DOG AND CAT GOODIE BAGS:

Bag it. Your first decision is what type of bag you want to use. Keep it simple by decorating brown paper bags with markers and stickers. But be sure to make it clear whether the bag will be for a canine or feline friend — you don't want anyone barking mad over a mouse squeak toy. Or you can use plastic goodie bags and decorate them with stickers or ribbons.

ollars. Shelter animals are often strays in need of a good home. One way to make sure they're never stray again is to give them a collar for their new identification tags. Have your guests bring collars of all izes, for dainty kittens all the way to Great Danes.

eashes. Cats seem to think leashes are beneath them, but dogs know a leash is a ticket to the great utdoors. Have your guests bring leashes in bright colors and patterns to set the mood for fun, frolicking dventure. After all, these shelter dogs are about to get a new leash on life!

oys. If any pets are in need of some serious fun, it's shelter animals. So add a few toys to each goodie ag to pump up the (bow) wow factor. From catnip chew rings and fishing-rod feather toys, to doggie tug-f-war pulls and floppy flying discs, you can brighten the lives of countless shelter animals.

Dog biscuits and cat treats. Pick up a box of dog treats and cat snacks from the store and seal hem in plastic storage bags. Add them to the goodie bags for a complete pet-care package!

MAKING A DOG OR CAT BED OUT OF OLD PILLOWCASES:

Have guests bring an old pillowcase from home.
Stuff the pillowcase with soft batting or old linens like blankets, sheets and towels.
With a grownup's help, use needle and thread to sew up the end of the pillowcase tight, making sure it's ealed securely. If there's a sewing machine handy, even better.
Test out the new pet beds to make sure they're soft and comfortable.

DECORATING CAT-CAKES:

They're purrrr-fectly delicious! Decorating cupcakes to look like kittens is a fun way to focus on animals, and the reward is sweet and tasty! Before your guests arrive, bake enough cupcakes for you and your friends to decorate at least one each. Use a simple box cake mix and paper cupcake liners. Once your cupcakes have cooled, you're ready to decorate.

Here's what you'll need to make cat-faced cupcakes:

Chocolate frosting
White frosting
Black gel icing pen
Chocolate chips
Starburst brand candy or pink taffy

DECORATING CAT-CAKES:

Spread the top of the cupcake with icing (either white or brown).
Place two chocolate chips for eyes and one for a nose.
Cut the pink Starburst in half, then roll them out into ovals and triangles to make small cat tongues and ears.

Place the pink tongue below the nose. Use the black gel icing pen to pipe half-circles between the nose and tongue to form the shape of a mouth.
Pipe black icing in lines from the nose to form cat's whiskers.
Press the pink triangles in place at the top of the face as cat ears.
Admire, eat and enjoy!

BAKING DOG BISCUITS TO TAKE HOME:

Here's a simple recipe for homemade dog biscuits. Once they've cooled, place them in a plastic storage bag or decorative tin, and take them home for the dogs in your life.

Bow-Wowie Biscuits

2 cups all-purpose flour
2 teaspoons baking powder
1 cup smooth peanut butter
1 cup half-n-half

Preheat the oven to **375** degrees.

1. In a large bowl, combine the flour and baking powder.

2. Using a handheld mixer (and with a grownup's help), blend in the peanut butter and half-n-half.

3. Place dough on a lightly floured surface and roll it out.

BAKING DOG BISCUITS

. We prefer a thicker biscuit, so make sure your dough is at least one-quarter inch thick.

. Using a cookie cutter shaped like a dog bone, cut out cookie shapes. Place onto a cookie sheet covered with parchment paper. Bake for 15 to 20 minutes until lightly brown.

Cool and serve to your favorite four-legged friends.

ONE PERSON MAKING A DIFFERENCE:

Animals in shelters certainly need help. But what about animals in the wild? **Joe Duff** was a professional photographer and amateur pilot when he became fascinated with whooping cranes, the majestic white birds that were disappearing from North America. In 1994, he put his interests together and teamed up with another pilot, **Bill Lishman**, to form **Operation Migration**. Bill had already been flying his ultra-light aircraft with geese, and they wanted to see what they could do to help the whooping cranes, whose population had dropped to just 15 birds by 1941. Joe and Bill wondered whether they could train the birds to follow the ultra-light planes and learn safer migratory routes. "You don't have to be a rocket scientist to help make a difference," explains Joe (pictured here). "You just have to want to do it, and to try. You'll be surprised how far you can take it." The first whooping crane flight took place in 2001, teaching a small flock how to migrate 1,200 miles from Wisconsin to Florida. They got there with eight whooping cranes — seven on the wing and one in a crate. Joe is excited to see the whooping cranes' numbers climbing, and by spring 2010, more than 100 birds made the return flight to Wisconsin from Florida. But he's even more excited about what Operation Migration has done to teach others about endangered animals. "With an ultra-light, you can save one whooping crane," Joe says. "But with education, you can save them all."

Learn more about Operation Migration online at www.OperationMigration.org.

FEBRUARY

Please come to...
A VALENTINE'S DAY PARTY!

What to bring:
Empty shoebox
Heart-shaped stickers, doilies & foam cutouts
Deck of cards
Coloring books or activity books

PUT YOUR HEART INTO IT!

Valentine's Day is the perfect time of year to brighten someone's world with a heart-warming card. And while it's great to let family and friends know how much you care, other folks might need some cheer, too. Consider throwing a special Valentine's Day party in your classroom at school and making Valentine's Day cards for children who are in the hospital. A colorful card with a hopeful message might be the perfect medicine to lift someone's spirits. And it could make you feel pretty good, too.

WHAT YOU CAN DO:

Throw a heart-themed party, from the food you serve to the projects you make to the decorations you hang. Here's a quick list of ideas:

1. **Create Valentine's Day cards for kids in a local hospital.**
2. **Make care boxes for children at a local crisis center or shelter.**
3. **Bake Valentine's Day cookies to sell at a school bake sale.**
4. **Decorate heart-themed picture frames.**
5. **Learn about Kiva Microfunds, and consider sending a valentine that keeps on giving.**

MAKING VALENTINE'S DAY CARDS FOR THE HOSPITAL:

Talk with your teacher to decide how and when you'll make the cards. And get permission to use some classroom supplies, along with the items your classmates contribute:

Construction paper
Glue
Markers
Scissors

- glitter pens and glitter glue
- Heart stickers and foam cutouts
- Heart-shaped doilies
- Pipe cleaners

Decorate your cards. Write uplifting messages like, "Hope you feel better!" and "Get well soon!" in your valentines. Remember that the children in the hospital might be nervous and frightened.

Contact the hospital's Volunteer Coordinator to determine when you can drop off the valentines.

Include your school's name, classroom teacher, a phone number and other contact information with the valentines before passing them on to the Coordinator.

With permission, the Volunteer Coordinator might let you pass the cards out.

Be sure to wear a friendly smile!

MAKING CARE BOXES FOR A SHELTER:

Have everyone bring in a shoe box from home.
Using the same supplies that you gathered for the Valentine's Day cards, decorate the shoe boxes with bright construction paper, hearts and doilies.
Once the glue has dried, fill the boxes with items that might cheer a child:

- Construction paper flowers
- Cookies set aside from the bake sale
- Deck of cards
- Coloring books
- Activity books
- Lists of jokes

And don't forget to make a special valentine with a personal note from you, and include that in the care box, too! Contact the Volunteer Coordinator at the crisis center or shelter to determine when you can drop off the care boxes.

BAKING VALENTINE'S COOKIES:

Be sure to get permission from your teacher or principal before planning a bake sale at school. And remember the basics:

Location, location, location. Look for high-traffic areas where you'll see the most potential customers: in the lobby before and after school, in the cafeteria at lunch.

Who are your customers? Most people on the go will want to grab something that's easy to eat. Think about selling one or two cookies together, rather than a whole dozen at a time.

Sweet-looking products. Package your products well, and customers will snatch them up. Try stacking two cookies together, wrapping them in plastic wrap and tying the ends with a curly red ribbon.

Love notes. When you set up your bake stand, don't forget to post a few signs telling people what it's about. Let them know the prices of your baked goods. But also tack up information about the charity that will benefit from the sale.

Manage your money. Start off with about $5 in small bills and quarters in a sealed container. That way you can give change to your early customers and build up from there.

Don't forget to set some of the cookies aside to give to people who might get overlooked, from custodians to cafeteria workers to librarians to the school nurse!

Here's our tried and true cookie recipe:

2 sticks (1 cup) butter, softened
¾ cup sugar
1 large egg yolk
¼ cup milk
2 teaspoons vanilla extract
2 ½ cups all-purpose flour
1 teaspoon baking powder
½ teaspoon salt

Decorate with a light icing glaze:
2 cups powdered sugar
3 tablespoon water
Food coloring

Preheat the oven to 350 degrees.

1. In a big bowl, beat the butter and sugar together with a handheld mixer (and an adult's help). Add the egg yolk, milk and vanilla. Beat until it's smooth. Add the flour, baking powder and salt. Mix everything together to form a soft dough.

2. Roll the dough into a big ball, then wrap it in plastic wrap and place it in the refrigerator for about 15 minutes.

3. Sprinkle a bit of flour onto a flat surface and roll the dough out. We like our cookies thick, so we recommend flattening the dough to about one-quarter inch thickness.

4. Using heart-shaped cookie cutters, cut out hearts and put them onto a baking sheet lined with parchment paper. Bake for 13 minutes or until golden brown. Let cool before decorating.

5. Mix the powdered sugar and water together in a bowl using a handheld mixer (and an adult's help). Add food coloring. Spread onto cookies with a butter knife. Add sprinkles and have fun!

MAKING HEART-THEMED FRAMES TO TAKE HOME:

Who's in your heart? You can show the world by making a heart-themed picture frame and inserting a photo of your favorite person. Here's how:

1. Gather enough photo frames for everyone participating. Frames can be inexpensive when purchased in bulk from hobby stores.

2. Glue heart-shaped beads, red and white buttons, or even foam cutouts onto your Valentine's Day frame. Or you can try using craft glue like Mod Podge brand and cover the entire frame in heart-themed paper.

Turn on some heart-pumping music while you decorate. You and your friends deserve to have a good time while you're doing good!

ONE PERSON MAKING A DIFFERENCE:

Sending a valentine each February is a great way to show you care. But how about sending one that keeps on giving, throughout the year? With a few simple steps, it's easy to reach out to people in need around the world. That's what **Matt Flannery** and **Jessica Jackley** discovered in 2004 after visiting East Africa. They saw firsthand how many poor families could be helped when small businesses there received grants as simple as $100. So Matt and Jessica started **Kiva**, a micro-lending website that connects people just like you with poor and struggling entrepreneurs around the globe. "We are more connected than we realize to people who seem very different from us and live on the other side of the world," says Matt. "With the help of the internet and technology, physical distance means little in the world today." After just five years in business, Kiva helped donors lend more than $100 million to people struggling to make a living in some of the poorest nations on Earth! The idea of microloans (lending small amounts of money) isn't just to take the $25 you might have in your piggy bank and donate it. It's to let donors choose where their $25 will go – whether to a banana seller in Uganda who dreams of building a house, or to a shoe seller in Mongolia who wants to pay for her son's education. And this is a loan: Unlike a typical donation, the money you give is paid back to you! So you can lend that $25 again and again and again. It's truly a valentine that keeps on giving! "Helping people is contagious," says Matt. "If you have an idea for a way to help people, talk about it! Others will want to help you and will get involved, too." That's how Kiva did it!

Learn more about Kiva by visiting their website at www.Kiva.org.

MARCH

Please come to...
A HELPING-HANDS PARTY!

What to bring:
New toothbrush
Comb or brush
Small box of bandages
Unopened toothpaste
Small shampoo
Anti-bacterial cream
Washcloth
Soap
Lip balm

LEND A HELPING HAND!

Life can be challenging, even in the best of times. But when disaster strikes, it can make day-to-day living that much harder. Whether it's a tornado in the United States or an earthquake in Asia, families around the globe can witness their lives change in a single day. You can help other children affected by these disasters by reaching out in simple but profound ways. Through a helping-hands party, you can send comfort packages to kids just like yourselves and let them know you care.

WHAT YOU CAN DO:

Throw a party and decorate with hand-shaped construction paper cutouts. Invite friends over to put together kits for children who have been hit by floods, earthquakes or other disasters. They can be distributed by relief agencies like the Red Cross. Before you begin, call your local Red Cross or other agency and let them know your plans. That way you can find out if there are specific needs (like mosquito spray or sun block), and you'll line up a contact person who will take your finished kits.

Here's a quick list of party ideas:

1. **Decorate canvas bags.**
2. **Assemble care kits.**
3. **Bake helping-hands shaped pretzels to eat together.**
4. **Make helping-hands T-shirts to take home.**
5. **Learn about World Bicycle Relief and how bikes are helping people in need.**

DECORATING CANVAS BAGS:

Select the style of bag you want to use. Back sacks with drawstrings are easy for kids to carry and ensure that the items placed inside will not fall out easily.

Place newspapers or cardboard inside the bag to prevent paint from seeping through to the other side.

Using fabric paint and stencils, decorate the bags in bright, cheery patterns that work for boys and for girls. Use stencils shaped like stars, moons, flowers and insects, and you'll create bags that are sure to please all kinds of kids.

Once the bags have dried, place the care kits inside.

ASSEMBLING THE CARE KITS:

Gather the basics. When a natural disaster hits, some of the ordinary tasks we take for granted – like brushing our teeth in the morning – become extraordinary challenges. Put together kits that meet basic daily needs, and you'll bring a tremendous comfort to kids in crisis.

Separate the items into even piles around your dining room table. Have your guests walk around the table and put each item into a gallon-size, re-sealable plastic bag (these plastic bags can serve many purposes after a disaster).

Have everyone take a moment to write a personal note to the child who will receive the bag. Those few little words of encouragement might be just the thing to help the child through.

Once the care kits are assembled and all the items are inside the plastic bags, place them into the decorated canvas bags and deliver them to your local Red Cross or other relief agency.

BAKING HELPING-HANDS SHAPED PRETZELS:

You and your friends deserve to celebrate all your efforts. What better way to enjoy each other's helping hands than by making fun, delicious hand-shaped pretzels? Here's how:

1 package (0.25 ounce) active dry-yeast
1 ½ cups warm water
1 teaspoon sugar
½ teaspoon salt
4 cups all-purpose flour
Olive oil
1 tablespoon baking soda
¼ cup warm water

1. At least one hour before your guests arrive, start the dough. Combine the warm water and yeast in a mixing bowl, along with the sugar and salt. Let it sit for about five minutes.

2. When everything has dissolved, add the flour.

3. Knead with your hands for about five minutes, until the dough loses its stickiness. Put a few drops of oil in a bowl and swirl it around to coat it. Then place your dough in the bowl, turning it a few times to lightly coat the whole dough ball in oil. Cover the bowl with a dry cloth and set it aside in a warm, dry place, allowing the dough to rise until it has doubled in size (about 1 hour).

4. When you and your friends are ready to make the pretzel hands, preheat the oven to 425 degrees.

5. Punch the dough down and divide it into 10 equal pieces. Lightly grease your hands to keep the dough from sticking. With the palms of your hands, roll each piece out into a long rope, about the width of your finger. Tear off one quarter of the rope and set it aside. Spiral the remaining longer rope onto a cookie sheet covered in parchment paper. Form a spiraled circle that represents the palm of your hand. With the rope you set aside, tear it into five small ropes to represent your fingers. Push them into place around your spiral palm.

6. Mix together the baking soda and warm water. Brush each hand completely with the mixture. Sprinkle with coarse salt and bake until browned, about 12 minutes.

Eat and enjoy all your handiwork!

MAKING HELPING-HANDS T-SHIRTS TO TAKE HOME:

You and your friends can decorate T-shirts to celebrate your helping-hands party. Just reuse the fabric paint from the canvas bag project. Only this time, you won't need any special stencils. You already have what you'll need on your body: your hands!

Here's what to do:
Gather enough plain white T-shirts for everyone in your group. Buying T-shirts in bulk helps save on the cost.
Slip newspapers or cardboard into the shirt to prevent paint from seeping through to the other side.
Dip your hands in the fabric paint.
Press your hands onto the T-shirts, forming patterns of your choice.
Repeat until you're satisfied. And have fun!

ONE COUPLE MAKING A DIFFERENCE:

When disaster strikes, what do people need most? That's what **Leah Missbach Day** and her husband, **F.K. Day**, asked themselves after a devastating tsunami struck the Indian Ocean in 2004. They already worked in the bicycle industry, so their minds naturally turned to bikes and how they could help. "The children there had lost so much – they needed clothing and books," Leah recalls, "but we loved bikes! Bikes give you joy, and we thought it would be a beautiful thing to give those kids a true sense of freedom and independence – return it to them." So they began **World Bicycle Relief**, assembling more than 24,000 sturdy bikes onsite and getting them into the hands of local people who needed them most. The bikes provided inexpensive transportation and allowed many of the parents in Sri Lanka and Indonesia to begin piecing their lives back together – getting their children back to school, returning to work, visiting a doctor. "The bicycle was the thing that instantly pulled that all together," Leah says. Now the organization distributes bikes to people in countries around the world, such as Zambia in Africa, where walking is the primary means of getting around. With a bicycle, a four-hour walk to see a doctor is cut to just one hour. What would you do if someone gave you three extra hours in your day? "Helping others is simply human. It makes you feel good," says Leah, who is looking ahead to World Bicycle Relief's next project to assemble and distribute 23,000 bikes to HIV/AIDS workers in Zambia. "My number one hope for the future is that the people we're serving also become hopeful."

Learn more about World Bicycle Relief at www.WorldBicycleRelief.org.

APRIL

Please come to...
AN EARTH-DAY PARTY!

What to bring:
Garden gloves
Unwanted jeans
Garbage bags
Fabric belt

WHAT YOU CAN DO:

1. **Clean up a local park or public area.**

2. **Become recycling ambassadors at your school.**

3. **Decorate an Earth Day cake.**

4. **Sew shopping bags out of old jeans.**

5. **Check out Surfrider Foundation, which helps protect the world's oceans and beaches.**

REDUCE, REUSE, RECYCLE AND REJOICE!

Earth Day is celebrated in the United States every April 22nd. You and your friends can help tackle environmental issues in your community and have fun learning more about problems that affect the planet by throwing an Earth Day party. Think big, think creative – but most of all, think green!

CLEANING UP A LOCAL PARK OR PUBLIC AREA:

Earth Day is a great holiday to celebrate in your classroom. With your teacher's permission, you can plan exciting activities both indoors and out. Start with taking a field trip to a park or public space in your community that needs a little help. Make sure everyone knows to wear their grubbies to school that day. Slip into your gardening gloves and start picking up all the junk you can find. Have everyone in your class grab a partner and form a "clean team," with one person carrying the trash bag and the other throwing in the trash. See which team collects the most garbage in 30 minutes.

BECOMING RECYCLING AMBASSADORS:

Why do we recycle? What can be recycled? What do the triangles mean on the bottom of plastic containers? You and your classmates can help the planet by spreading the word about recycling. Check out books about trash and landfills, and learn everything you can. Invite an expert into your classroom to help give you more information. Then write up posters explaining what you've learned. With permission from your principal or teacher, hang the posters around school. Once you become masters on the topic, visit classrooms throughout your school to teach other students even more about recycling issues.

You can also try starting a No-Waste Lunch program at your school. Disposable food and drink containers, plastic utensils, and wrappings all create incredible amounts of garbage in school lunchrooms every day.

You can encourage your classmates to make a change. Here are some suggestions:
Pack reusable, refillable drink containers
Pack whole fruit when possible
Use stainless steel spoons and forks instead of plastic
Put sandwiches and snacks in reusable containers instead of disposable baggies

DECORATING AN EARTH DAY CAKE:

What better way to celebrate the planet's big day than with a special cake? Bake and bring in an unfrosted sheet cake. Break your class up into teams that will help cover the Earth.

Ocean team: Mix up blue icing to represent water. Spread onto the whole cake.

Green team: Once the "water" is on the cake, you need to put on the land.
Mix up a bowl of green icing to represent the seven continents. Have a globe or map nearby to help get them in the right place.

Animals team: Use icing fondant to roll out animal shapes.
Form elephants, dolphins, penguins and tigers — all sorts of wild animals — by molding the fondant with your hands. Place on the continents or in the water.

Plants team: Use icing fondant to form flowers, palm trees, cacti and more by molding the fondant with your hands. Place them on the continents.

Dig in: Once you're done decorating, slice up, serve and enjoy your little piece of the world!

SEWING BAGS OUT OF OLD JEANS TO TAKE HOME:

Everybody has heard the question, "Paper or plastic?" Next time you're at the grocery store, tell them, "Denim!" With just a few simple passes on a sewing machine, you can refashion an old pair of blue jeans into a great bag for carrying your groceries, your school books, or anything you need for an afterschool activity.

Here's how:
With your teacher's permission, ask classmates who can sew or whose parents can sew to bring in a sewing machine. Just one or two will do the trick.

Have everyone in class bring in one pair of old, unwanted jeans. They can be any size — whether for adults or kids.

Cut off the legs of the jeans in a straight line near the crotch.

Cut along the inseam, up one leg, across the crotch, and down the other leg.

Turn the jeans inside out.

SEWING JEANS BAG

Pin the bottom edge together in a straight line. This will form the base of the jeans bag.

Using a sewing machine, sew straight across the bottom of the bag following the pins. Sew again, to reinforce stitches and ensure the bag's strength. Cut away excess fabric.

Pin the fabric belt to the sides of the jeans along the tops, near the belt loops. You might need to cut off any metal holds from the belt. Fold about one inch of the belt under at each end before pinning.

Sew the belt ends onto the sides of the jeans in a box shape to ensure strength.

Turn the jeans back from inside out, and voila! You have a sturdy, cool messenger bag!

ONE PERSON MAKING A DIFFERENCE:

Surfer **Glenn Hening** was at the beach in Malibu, California, back in 1984 when he began to worry. Manmade forces were changing the shape of the waves, ruining a popular surfing beach. He wanted to do something about it, so he called on surfers **Lance Carson** and **Tom Pratte** for help. "What we wanted to do was change one little thing," Glenn says. They brought surfers together to confront the issues they were facing, forming a strong community they called the **Surfrider Foundation**. Since that time, their idea has grown into an organization with over 50,000 members and 90 chapters around the world. From testing coastal and lake waters for pollution to cleaning up garbage-strewn beaches to preventing erosion, the Surfrider Foundation works to protect the Earth's oceans, waves and beaches for all of us. "Do everything you can – even if it's just something small – every chance you get," Glenn advises, emphasizing how important it is to stay informed. "Be passionate, and also patient, and know your facts. These are the keys to creating change."

Learn more about the Surfrider Foundation at www.Surfrider.org.

MAY

Please come to...
A PLANTING PARTY!

What to bring:
Flower seedlings
Gardening gloves
Shovels or spades
One-gallon milk jug, rinsed

WHAT YOU CAN DO:

You can help a local community center or low-income daycare look brighter by volunteering to plant flowers and shrubs. A local public school might be another site that needs some spiffing up with colorful blooms. Or you could take it a step further by putting together a vegetable garden at your own school. Talk to your teacher and principal first; then you and your friends can pledge to really mind your peas and q's! Here's a quick list of ideas:

1. **Plant flowers at a community center, daycare or public school.**
2. **Create milk jug birdhouses to invite feathery friends.**
3. **Make delicious dirt cake with worms.**
4. **Decorate sunhats with plastic bugs, flowers and fabric glue.**
5. **Learn about Growing Power, Will Allen's urban farming efforts.**

GROW WITH IT!

Flowers are a great way to dress up a neighborhood. And planting vegetables and herbs promises a bounty of healthy produce to come. When you think of ideas to make your community look better, remember that the best way to beautify is to get down and dirty. And May is the perfect time of year to put your hands into the soil and plant a garden.

PLANTING FLOWERS:

Before you even send out the invitations, make sure you line up all the details you need to ensure a successful planting party. Contact the Volunteer Coordinator at the daycare or community center to determine what needs to be done and when to do it. Invite her to participate too, and be sure there's a hose on hand to give those thirsty flowers a drink. Find out what types of flowers would work well in the space provided – shade-loving begonias or sun-hogging daisies?

Gather up all the flowers you and your friends have supplied. Organize by height, color or watering needs.

Break the group into teams so that when you get to the garden site, you're ready for action.

Slip on those gardening gloves, grab the shovels and spades, and start planting!

CREATING MILK JUG BIRDHOUSES:

What's a garden without a party? Invite feathery friends to come dine and roost with creative milk jug birdhouses.

Here's how to do it:

1. Wash out a one-gallon milk jug and let it dry. Be sure to save the cap.

2. Have an adult cut out a three-by-five-inch rectangle on two facing sides. Start the rectangle at least two inches from the bottom. This way the seeds won't spill out when the birds perch on the sides to eat.

3. Now you're ready to decorate. Using permanent markers, draw whatever you'd like onto the plastic jug: geometric shapes, illustrations of birds, even ivy.

4. Poke a hole on two opposite sides of the jug's neck. Pass a 10-inch string through the holes; then tie the ends together in a knot.

Now you're ready to hang your feeder. Pick a tree, pack the bottom with birdseed and let the party start!

MAKING DIRT CAKE WITH WORMS:

What better way to celebrate all your garden work than with a delicious dirt cake?
Serve it in a flower pot and top it off with some gummy worms and a bright flower – naturally!
Follow this recipe:

1 (16 ounce) package chocolate cookies
2 (5 ounce) packages of instant chocolate pudding
6 cups milk
1 package gummy worms
1 New, clean flower pot
Long-stemmed flowers

1. Line the inside of the flower pot with plastic wrap. Crush the cookies to a fine, dirtlike texture and set them aside.

2. Mix the chocolate pudding with the milk; set aside until pudding is the proper consistency.

3. Fill the pot with all the pudding. Sprinkle the top of the pudding with crumbled cookies so it looks like dirt.

4. Pop flowers into the pot and arrange gummy worms.

Serve, squirm and enjoy!

DECORATING SUN HATS TO TAKE HOME:

Before you venture out to the garden, make sure you're covered. As in, your head. You and your friends can have a little fun making wacky, worm covered hats to wear to your big dig.

Here's how:

1. Pass out a hat to each of your friends. When you purchase in bulk, you can keep the costs down.

2. Place piles of garden-themed gizmos on the table, from the heads of silk flowers to plastic insects, frogs and wiggly worms.

DECORATING SUN HATS TO TAKE HOME:

3. With the help of an adult, use a glue gun to affix the decorations onto the hats.

4. Let the hats sit undisturbed until the glue dries.

When they're ready, pop them on and head off for a day of fun in the sun!

ONE PERSON MAKING A DIFFERENCE:

What if you never heard the crunchy snap of a fresh carrot? Many kids living in poor, urban areas don't get the chance to taste fresh fruits and vegetables. They live in "food deserts," neighborhoods that lack grocery stores where fresh produce is sold. **Will Allen** wanted to change that. "You're not going to get good food at fast-food restaurants or corner stores," Will says. "People are trapped in these communities without access to healthy food." Will had grown up on a farm, and in 1993, he bought up the last working farm in his town of Milwaukee, Wisconsin. When kids from a local YWCA wanted help planting an organic garden, he decided to help them learn about raising fresh vegetables and distributing them to the community. Other people heard about his efforts, and by 1995, **Growing Power** was born. "I'm not a person who's going to sit in an office all day," says Will, who teaches people from around the world his organic farming practices. "I want my hands in the soil." Growing Power has taken root over the years, expanding into 10 farms that distribute healthy produce to more than 10,000 people throughout Wisconsin and the Chicago area. Bit by bit – and bite by bite – Will is showing the next generation how to grow healthy food for their families and their communities. "My personal goal is that everyone has access to good, healthy food – regardless of their financial situation," says Will. "We can end world hunger by developing local food systems. It's a revolution."

Learn more about Will Allen and Growing Power at www.GrowingPower.org.

JUNE

Please come to...

A LEMONADE STAND PARTY!

What to bring:
Lemons
Cups
Cardboard and markers to make signs

IT MAY BE HOT, BUT YOU'RE COOL!

Yes, it's hot outside. But you can keep cool and be cool by hosting a lemonade stand! And to help keep business brisk, you can make a craft to sell at your stand, too. What better way to spend a summer afternoon than hanging out with friends while raising money for a good cause? Sweet!

WHAT YOU CAN DO:

1. Host a lemonade stand.
2. Create magnet picture frames to sell.
3. Make lemon ice in lemon cones.
4. Decorate cool sunglasses to wear while you work.
5. Check out Alex's Lemonade Stand, and learn about how one little girl has raised millions of dollars.

HOSTING A LEMONADE STAND:

Throwing a lemonade stand party is fun and easy. But you should remember a few tips to guarantee a steady stream of customers:

Right place: It's important to choose a spot where you will see plenty of potential customers. Find a place where lots of people are walking by, but make sure it's close to your house so you can easily set up or grab extra supplies.

Right time: An important thing to think about is the time of day. When are people feeling thirsty? At lunchtime? Or in the late afternoon, walking home from school or work? And watch the calendar for a special event in your area. Anytime there are extra people around — whether at an art fair or a book festival — sales are sure to skyrocket!

HOSTING A LEMONADE STAND:

Read the signs: Grab some pens, paint, glitter and other art supplies to make signs that will attract customers to your stand. Tell folks what you're selling (lemonade!) and how much it costs. Hang signs at nearby street corners to encourage customers to walk over to your stand. And don't forget to make a poster about the organization you're raising money for: People like to learn about groups doing good work, and it just might inspire them to give an extra donation!

Supplies: You won't need much! Besides a stack of paper (not plastic!) cups to serve your lemonade in, you'll need a table and a few chairs, as well as a box to hold your money. Be sure to start with a few small bills and coins so you're ready to provide change to your early customers.

Simple lemonade recipe
8-10 fresh lemons
1 cup sugar
6 cups water

Juice the lemons to make one cup of juice. Before you squeeze the lemons, roll them firmly on the counter with your hands to soften them.

In a one-gallon plastic pitcher, combine lemon juice, sugar and cold water. Stir, chill and serve over ice. Delicious!

CREATING MAGNET PICTURE FRAMES:

Sometimes the weather doesn't always heat up enough to keep sales scorching. To boost revenue, try making a summer craft like a decorated magnet picture frame. Tell your customers they can hang it right on the refrigerator to be reminded of their summer fun every day of the year!

Here's how:

Magnet frame kits are available at most craft stores. Buying in bulk keeps the cost down.

Using foam shapes, glue bright suns, flowers, beach balls and other patterns onto the frame. Spell out words like "summer!" and "fun!" to go along with it.

Use glitter pens or glue on plastic jewels to make the frames sparkle.

Once the frames have dried, you're ready to start selling!

MAKING LEMON ICE IN LEMON CONES:

You and your friends will need a sweet treat to help you keep cool during your lemonade stand. But you don't want to drink all your inventory! So make sure to whip up a lemony treat that's alright to eat while you're outside. And who needs to use a cup when you can serve it in one of your lemons? Here's how:

Start by making lemon ice ahead of time. Then let your guests spoon it into the lemon cones before going outside.

2 cups freshly squeezed lemon juice (about 20 fresh lemons)
½ cup lemon zest
3 cups sugar
3 cups water
1 unsqueezed lemon for every guest

Get a grownup's help for this part:

1. Combine sugar and water in a saucepan over medium heat until the sugar dissolves. Stir in the lemon zest, and keep stirring until it comes to a boil. Remove from the heat and let it cool.
Then add the lemon juice.

2. Pour the liquid into a freezer-safe container, and pop it into the freezer until it turns solid.

3. When you and your guests are ready to cool off, get the lemon cones ready. Count how many guests you have, and pull aside that many lemons. Cut off the top third of the lemons and hollow out the insides. Be careful not to cut through the lemon skin.

4. To help the lemons stand upright, cut off a bit of the thick peel at the bottom of each lemon – but again make sure you don't puncture the lemon skin. Pass around a scoop and fill the cones with the yummy lemon ice. Your bright yellow cones are the ultimate "green" dessert!

DECORATING SUNGLASSES TO TAKE HOME:

The lemon ice will help you keep cool. Now do a craft project that will have you looking cool. Try making crazy sunglasses to wear while you work the lemonade stand. Use the same foam and jewel decorations you used for the magnet picture frames. Glue on some feathers or twisted pipe cleaners to make especially outlandish designs. Sunglasses are available in bulk at your local craft store, too.

ONE PERSON MAKING A DIFFERENCE:

Alex Scott wasn't even one year old when she was diagnosed with cancer. After receiving treatment at a hospital when she was four, Alex told her parents that she wanted to have a lemonade stand. She wanted to raise money so her doctors could find a cure for all childhood cancer. "When she said she was going to do a stand and raise money, I told her it was going to be hard," recalls Alex's mom, **Liz Scott.** "Her attitude was, 'I don't care, I'll do it anyway' – that whole idea that if you believe you can do something, don't let anyone tell you that you can't." Liz and husband **Jay Scott** gave their OK, and Alex raised $2,000! She went on to hold lemonade stands each year, and her story inspired other children around the world to do the same. Alex died in 2004 at the age of eight, but in her brief lifetime, she raised over one million dollars! Since that very first stand, the **Alex's Lemonade Stand Foundation** – which her family started to honor her name and her fighting spirit – has raised over $30 million to help battle childhood cancer. "Our goal is to always have kids involved," Liz says, "holding stands and raising money – and helping other kids."

Learn more about Alex's story at www.AlexsLemonade.org.

JULY

Please come to...
A SPORTS PARTY!

What to bring:
New or gently used sports equipment

HIT A HOME RUN!

Sports are a fun part of being a kid. You get to learn new skills, run around with your friends and get great exercise! Almost all sports require some equipment. Do you have any spare basketballs or soccer balls at your house? Or a few more jump ropes than you can use? Host a sports party and donate your gently used equipment, and you'll hit a homerun with kids who can't afford their own.

WHAT YOU CAN DO:

Decorate your party in a sports theme. And get creative with your invitations: cut them out in the shape of a ball or baseball glove or cleat. Game stats on the back can show the party details (the where, when and why). Make sure you include a list of the type of equipment you are looking for. Here are some party ideas:

1. **Collect used sports equipment to donate to needy kids.**
2. **Participate in a walkathon.**
3. **Work up a sweat making homemade ice cream.**
4. **Decorate jerseys with stencils of your favorite sports.**
5. **Check out Sports Gift, which recycles gently used equipment for needy kids.**

COLLECTING USED SPORTS EQUIPMENT:

Send the invitations out early so your guests have enough time to gather equipment.

Here are some examples of what guests can bring:

Baseballs	**Tennis balls**
Softballs	**Shin guards**
Mitts	**Basketballs**
Bats	**Footballs**
Jump ropes	**Ball pumps**
Tennis rackets	**Cleats**
Soccer balls	**Frisbees**

COLLECTING USED SPORTS EQUIPMENT:

You and your friends can dig through your garages or basements and clean out what you don't use anymore (this is the part Mom will love!). Look for the sports equipment you either outgrew or replaced. On the party day, make sure you have boxes ready to collect all of the equipment you and your friends have gathered. Once you're finished, take the boxes to a local charity that could use them. Or seal the boxes and mail them to a charity that accepts used sports equipment.

PARTICIPATING IN A WALKATHON:

Another great way to have fun with your friends and help a good cause is by participating in a walkathon. Most events have special routes for kids under 12. Older kids are usually allowed to participate in the longer walks with an adult. Here's what you should know:

1. Signing up: For some walkathons, participants pay an entrance fee, and the money goes directly to charity. Others require participants to get a certain number of pledges. A pledge is when a sponsor agrees to pay a certain amount of money for each mile you walk. So if someone pledges $5 for every mile, and you walk five miles, you'll raise $25 for charity!

2. Getting Sponsors: To find sponsors, ask neighbors and family friends. Let folks know they can pledge whatever amount they are comfortable with – every little bit helps!

PARTICIPATING IN A WALKATHON:

3. Dressing for success: The day of the walk, make sure to check the weather and dress appropriate You'll need your most comfortable shoes, a hat to keep your head cool, and don't forget sun block. Once you're set to go, you'll really put your best foot forward!

WORKING UP A SWEAT MAKING ICE CREAM:

You and your friends might be ready for a break, but you don't have to take a timeout on the fun. Prepare a sweet and delicious treat of ice cream in a bag, and you'll really score with your guests!

Here's what you'll need:
1 gallon-size plastic baggie with sealable top
1 quart-size plastic baggie with sealable top
3 cups crushed ice
¼ cup rock salt
½ cup milk (we use skim)
½ cup heavy whipping cream
2 tablespoons sugar
½ teaspoon vanilla

1. Fill the gallon-size baggie with ice and rock salt.

2. Fill the quart-size baggie with milk, cream, sugar and vanilla.

3. Seal the smaller baggie tightly and place it inside the larger baggie

4. Seal the larger baggie tightly.

5. Holding onto the top of the baggie, get moving! Shake, slide and bounce your concoction (without bursting the baggie open!) for 15 minutes.

6. When the ice cream looks like a smooth consistency, gently open the baggies. Pour the ice cream from the smaller baggie into a bowl, and dump out the ice-salt mixture from the larger baggie.

Keep things green by reusing the baggies. This recipe makes about two scoops per baggie. And you don't have to let the sports theme end there! Serve stadium food like peanuts (check for allergies), pretzels, hotdogs and Cracker Jack brand candy. Use a green cover for your table and mark off the yard lines with white tape so it looks like a football field. Place a whistle and a sports drink at each plate.

Let your imagination run wild!

DECORATING A JERSEY TO TAKE HOME:

Everybody loves to play, and what better way to show the world your favorite sports than to wear a painted jersey? Whether you're a soccer fan, football maniac or baseball junkie, you can declare your devotion with a brightly stenciled jersey.

Here's how:
Gather enough jerseys for all your guests. Buying in bulk can keep the costs down.

Using sports stencils and fabric paint, decorate the jerseys with your favorite sports images, from soccer balls and baseball bats to cleats and basketball hoops.

Using alphabet or number stencils, spell out your last name on the back of your jersey – just like the pros! Or paint on the number of your favorite athlete.

Let the jerseys dry; then pull them on and get out there and play!

ONE COUPLE MAKING A DIFFERENCE:

When **Keven Baxter** was a boy, he loved playing all kinds of sports. He grew up and had kids of his own who loved them too, and suddenly their house was filled with soccer balls, cleats and bright uniforms. And his neighbors' houses were the same. So Keven and his wife, **Claire Baxter**, decided to do something with all that equipment. They organized a collection at their local soccer league so families could donate their old gear. The Baxters boxed up the gently used balls, uniforms and cleats, and drove them down to Mexico to an orphanage where they'd helped out in the past. "If you see a need," Keven says, "just go and fill the need, whether it's giving one soccer ball or one book to one person. Because every little bit you do helps. " When Keven and Claire saw the faces of the kids who received the jerseys and other sports items, they knew they'd hit on something special. So they began to build on the idea, getting more people in their community involved. And before they knew it, **Sports Gift** was born. "Just do that one little bit you see in front of you, and that bit will grow," Keven says. That's what happened with Sports Gift: Since it began in 2002, the charity has donated more than 143,000 pieces of sporting equipment – cleats, balls, uniforms, mitts, bats, racquets, shin guards, playground items and more – to children around the world. Sports Gift does its part for the environment, too: They've recycled over 75,000 pounds of sports equipment, keeping it out of landfills while providing gear to over 100,000 children in need. "I have learned so many great lessons from playing sports," says Keven, "and I want all children to have that opportunity."

Learn more about Sports Gift at www.SportsGift.org.

AUGUST

Please come to...
A BOOKWORM PARTY!

What to bring:
One favorite children's book, wrapped in gift wrap
One favorite children's book, unwrapped

Please bring to a
**Bookworm
Party**

1. Favorite
Children's book
(wrapped)

2. Favorite
Children's book
(unwrapped)

PLAN FOR
A HAPPY

ENDING!

It's no mystery: Reading is one of the most important things you'll ever learn to do. Reading lets you learn, explore and enjoy life! But some children grow up without many books in their lives. You can share the joy of reading with other kids by throwing a bookworm party. Invite your friends over and ask them to bring a book to share with a needy group, like a crisis center. And before you know it, you'll write your own happy ending for a hungry reader.

WHAT YOU CAN DO:

Decorate your party in a book theme – you can even send out invitations on bookmarks. Use pages from old books to make place cards or fun decorations. Serve up a delicious treat based on a classic children's story.

1. **Collect books to give to a local crisis center.**
2. **Decorate a bookshelf to donate along with the books.**
3. **Bake and decorate a character from a favorite kids' story: The Gingerbread Man.**
4. **Make your own bookmarks and exchange books with each other.**
5. **Check out Heart of America Foundation, which puts books into the hands of kids who really need them.**

COLLECTING BOOKS TO GIVE TO CHARITY:

Gather up the unwrapped books that you and your friends have brought. You can put out a box near your front door and have them place the unwrapped books inside when they arrive. Or put the box out once everyone has settled in, and as everyone takes a turn putting their book in the box, ask them to share why they've chosen to contribute that story.

DECORATING A BOOKSHELF TO DONATE:

There has to be somewhere to put all these books you're donating. So along with the terrific new stories, why not donate a bookshelf to hold them? Just take an old bookshelf purchased at a second-hand store or even one your family doesn't need anymore. Be sure it's sturdy, then get to work giving it new life. Here's how:

Freshen up: You and your friends can grab some brushes and a can of paint, and with just a few coats, your bookcase will be reborn!

Dress up: Take a few of your old picture books and cut out your favorite illustrations. Using craft glue, attach the illustrations to the bookcase's sides and top. Let dry.

Polish up: Using a water-based acrylic varnish, cover the bookcase entirely. Let it dry, then stand back and admire your work!

BAKING GINGERBREAD MEN:

When you're hungry for adventure, you can pick up a book. When you're just plain hungry, you can pick up a cookbook! Why not mix the two together and cook a delicious character from a timeless children's story? Run, run, as fast as you can, and start baking your very own gingerbread man!

Our favorite gingerbread cookie recipe

3 cups all-purpose flour
½ teaspoon baking soda
½ teaspoon salt
2 teaspoons ground ginger
1 teaspoon ground cinnamon
¼ teaspoon ground cloves

¼ teaspoon ground nutmeg
1 stick unsalted butter
1 egg
½ cup brown sugar
¾ cup molasses

1. Before your guests come, mix up the dough. In one bowl, mix the dry ingredients.

2. In a second bowl, use a handheld mixer (and an adult's help) to blend the butter, egg, brown sugar and molasses.

3. Add the dry ingredients to the wet and mix thoroughly. Form a ball, cover and refrigerate for at least three hours.

4. When you are ready to bake your gingerbread cookies, have a grownup preheat the oven to 350 degrees. Line a baking sheet with parchment paper.

5. Sprinkle a bit of flour onto a clean, smooth work surface, and roll the dough out to about one-quarter inch thickness. Use cookie cutters to form your gingerbread man (and woman!) shapes. A spatula can help move the cookies onto the baking sheet.

6. Bake for about 10 minutes, depending on size. Smaller cookies may take less time, larger cookies a few more minutes.

7. Decorate with icing pens, bright candies and gumdrops, and eat up your cookie creation before he gets away!

MAKING BOOKMARKS AND EXCHANGING BOOKS TO TAKE HOME:

When the plot thickens, don't let yourself get lost! Keep track of your story with a beautiful bookmark that you create yourself. There are lots of ways to make bookmarks, so use your imagination to build one that unique!

Here's how:

1. Use stiff card stock. Cut out a rectangle that is about 2 inches by 6 inches.
2. Decorate with markers, stickers and ink stamps.
3. Use the back of your bookmark to write down some of your favorite books.
4. Once you're done, use clear shelf liner to laminate the front and back sides.
5. Punch a hole in the top with a hole puncher.
6. Thread a piece of ribbon through the hole. Pull the two ends together and tie a knot.

When you're ready to exchange books, have everyone sit in a big circle and hold the gift-wrapped book they brought from home. Ask one person to pick a magic number between one and 10. Then have everyone pass their book to the person on their left that many times. So if seven is your magic number, pass around the books seven times. Once you're done passing, everyone should be holding onto a brand new book. Stop, tear open the wrapping paper and start reading!

ONE COUPLE MAKING A DIFFERENCE:

Angie and **Bill Halamandaris** were already working with charity groups helping others when they saw a glaring problem. Children living in poor neighborhoods with struggling schools had few – if any – books to read. So they set out to change that. "Books are such a critical tool for kids to succeed in life," says Angie. Believing literacy and service learning go hand-in-hand, Angie and Bill began **Heart of America Foundation** in 1997 with the goal of building a nation of readers committed to volunteering. Not only have they given away more than 1.8 million books, Heart of America has also introduced more than 500,000 young people to the idea of helping their communities. In poor neighborhoods around the country, Heart of America volunteers are distributing books, creating cozy reading spaces in community centers and transforming elementary school libraries. "The library should be the heart and soul of the school," says Angie. "It's the place where students and their families can come. If we can revitalize it, then we feel like we've revitalized that community." So what do Angie and Bill have to say to kids who want to help out? "If you see something that concerns you," says Bill, "ask yourself, 'What am I going to do about it?' Whenever you respond – however big or small – it changes you for life. And the lives of those around you."

Find out more about the Heart of America Foundation at www.HeartofAmerica.org.

SEPTEMBER

Please come to...

A BACK-TO-SCHOOL PARTY!

What to bring:

Lunch box

And as many of the following items as possible to pack bags for kids who need extra help getting off to a good start in school!

Lined paper
Pens and pencils
Erasers
Highlighters
Dry-erase markers
Paperclips
Binders
Staples and stapler
Construction paper
Glue sticks
Markers
Tape
Art supplies
Backpacks

WHAT YOU CAN DO:

1. Pack bags of school supplies.
2. Make wacky pencil toppers.
3. Share school-lunch munching ideas.
4. Decorate water bottles for your own lunch box.
5. Check out Mr. Holland's Opus Foundation, which donates musical instruments to school kids around the country.

PACKING BAGS OF SCHOOL SUPPLIES:

What supplies should you ask your guests to bring? One of the best places to look is your own school supply list. There are many standard supplies common to all schools: paper, pens, pencils, markers and glue sticks. Send the party invitation – along with the wish list of helpful items – early enough so that your guests can get extra supplies while they're getting their own.

READY, SET, SCHOOL!

You've shopped for new clothes. Your books and pens are all packed. You're ready to go back to school! But some children aren't so lucky. They don't have all the supplies they need for learning. Try packing up school-supply bags to donate to a needy school in your area. And keep in mind that it could even be for your school. Ask your principal if there are families at your school who might benefit from a supply-packing party. If not, your principal can connect you with another school in your area that might need the help.

PACKING BAGS OF SCHOOL SUPPLIES:

Once you've collected all the supplies, sort them into piles. Put all the paper in one pile, all the markers in another and so on. Ask each of your guests to take a bag and work her way around the table, taking one item from every pile until each bag is full of supplies. When your bags are filled and ready, contact the principal or a designated teacher before you drop them off. The school can quietly make sure that the supply bags will reach the students who need them most!

MAKING WACKY PENCIL TOPPERS:

Creative writing takes on a whole new meaning with wacky and fun pencil toppers. Just set aside one or two extra packages of new pencils, and let your imaginations roam!

Here's what to do:

Wrap the top two inches of the pencil end with colorful pipe cleaners. Spiral to the pencil end, around the eraser. Leave one inch of pipe cleaner sticking up.

Dab the end of the pipe cleaner with glue and attach colorful pompons.

Glue craft eyes to the pompons. Cut out felt shapes for a nose, beak or mouth.

Include the pencil and pencil topper in your school-supply bag. You're setting some lucky student off on a fun and imaginative school year!

SHARING SCHOOL-LUNCH MUNCHING IDEAS:

After all that work, you and your guests will have worked up an appetite. And now that school is starting, it's time to think about packing school lunches. Here's where the lunch box you asked your guests to bring comes in:

Set out a variety of breads, from pita to multi-grain to flat wraps. Also put down a platter of lunch meat varieties, cream cheeses, hummus and dried fruits. And don't forget to offer different fresh fruits and veggies.

Ask your guests to circle the table and make up a few small sandwiches, encouraging them to try new things. They should fill up their lunch boxes with a little bit of everything.

Once everyone has tried all the offerings, sit down together at the table and eat lunch — just like at school. Only this time, you and your guests might have a few new ideas for what to pack during the school year!

DECORATING WATER BOTTLES TO TAKE HOME:

Kids like you keep busy schedules during the school year, with activities from morning to night. What better way to quench your thirst than with your own, personalized water bottle? When purchased in bulk, you can keep the cost down. Just make sure that everyone in the group has one, then break out the permanent markers. Draw butterflies, polka dots or write your name in bright colors.

Pack your bottle in your lunchbox and save on buying throwaway bottles of juice, soda or water. Cheers to you!

ONE PERSON MAKING A DIFFERENCE:

What makes for a great school year? Having classes with your favorite friends, for one thing. But also having terrific teachers, too. The 1995 movie *Mr. Holland's Opus* was about a music teacher who inspired his students to try their best. **Michael Kamen** was the real-life musician who wrote the score for that popular film. Music was his life, and to help ensure that all school children got a chance to learn music like he did, he created the **Mr. Holland's Opus Foundation**. "Michael grew up in New York public schools with strong music and arts programs," says **Felice Mancini**, the foundation's executive director. "He wanted to give back to the system that educated him and give back to other kids as well." Mr. Holland's Opus Foundation donates new and refurbished musical instruments to school children so that everyone – rich or poor – can have a chance to play violins, cellos, drums and more. Reaching an average of 10,000 children each year in schools and after-school programs around the United States, Michael's dream to share his passion for music keeps on growing. "He had a very big heart," Felice says about Michael, who died in 2003. "He felt bad that some kids who couldn't afford it were left out. Our goal is to make sure that no child goes through an education without having this incredible experience of making music."

Learn more about the Mr. Holland's Opus Foundation at www.MHOpus.org.

OCTOBER

Please come to...
A HALLOWEEN PARTY!

What to bring:
Pumpkin
Shoebox

Halloween Party

WHAT YOU CAN DO:

A Halloween party is a great way to raise spirits. Try hanging up ghostly good decorations and playing some eerie music, and you'll certainly set the mood for a boo-tiful party. Here's a quick list of ideas:

1. **Decorate pumpkins to take to a nearby senior center.**

2. **Make delicious treats for your local firefighters and police officers.**

3. **Bake spooky ghost hotdogs.**

4. **Create trick-or-treat bags to carry on your big night.**

5. **Check out the Pajama Program, which helps needy kids go to bed with simple comforts.**

SO FUN, IT'S SCARY!

Halloween is already one of the most fun-filled holidays of the year. But you can scare up even more excitement by throwing a party to help your community. Consider decorating pumpkins to deliver to your local senior center. And use some new tricks to whip up special treats for agencies that help keep your community safe, like the police and fire departments.

DECORATING PUMPKINS:

First call your neighborhood senior center to let them know your plans. Then have all your guests bring a pumpkin to the party. You provide the decorations:

• foam stick-on shapes
• glitter glue
• acrylic paints
• feathers

DECORATING PUMPKINS:

Set everything out on a table, and let the creativity flow. Add a little mood music, and you're in for a spooktacular session. But keep in mind that the finished pumpkins will be going to seniors, so keep the designs cheerful and fun, rather than gory!

When your pumpkins are ready, contact the Volunteer Coordinator at the senior center to determine the best time for dropping off your gorgeous gourds.

MAKING TREATS FOR FIREFIGHTERS AND POLICE:

Before your guests arrive, bake a few dozen batches of cupcakes using paper liners and box mixes (we prefer one box chocolate and one box white cake) and let them cool. When you're ready to decorate, pull them out and let the fun begin. Try making candy-corn goblins and marshmallow ghouls. There's no trick to making these treats.

Here's how:

1 (1 pound) box of powdered sugar
1 (8 ounce) brick of cream cheese
1 teaspoon vanilla
Green food coloring
Candy corns
Mini-marshmallows
Chocolate chips
Chocolate sprinkles

Using a handheld mixer (and a grownup's help), blend the powdered sugar, cream cheese, vanilla and green food coloring in a bowl. Spread it on the cupcakes.

Arrange candy corns in a row along the bottom face of the cupcake face to form jagged teeth.

Take two small marshmallows to use as eyes. Heat chocolate chips for just a few seconds to warm, then press onto the center of each marshmallow to form a pupil. Push the marshmallow eyes into the icing.

For hair, spread chocolate sprinkles along the top of the cupcake face.

When you are ready to make your cupcake delivery, simply line a few shoeboxes with aluminum foil and gently place your tricky treats inside.

BAKING GHOST HOTDOGS:

You and your friends are sure to be hungry after all that work. Serve a frighteningly good snack with hotdogs that look like ghosts.

Here's how:

1. Cut hotdogs in half (do not cut lengthwise).

2. Using store-bought dough for dinner rolls, such as Pillsbury brand crescent rolls, wrap the hotdog half in dough. Let excess dough drape around the base of the hotdog to help stand it up on an ungreased cookie sheet.

3. Create two eyes and an open mouth by using three black peppercorns.

Bake hotdogs standing upright at 350 degrees for 11 to 13 minutes.

CREATING TRICK-OR-TREAT BAGS TO TAKE HOME:

Decorate canvas bags with spooky themes, and make your Halloween night a howling good time. Keep the cost down by purchasing bags in bulk.

Here's what you can do:

Place a book or newspaper inside the bag to prevent ink from seeping onto the opposite sides of your bag.

Use fabric markers to draw pumpkins, ghosts and witches.

Make your images especially eerie by sewing on big, button eyes.

Don't forget your bag when you head out for trick-or-treating!

ONE PERSON MAKING A DIFFERENCE:

When the trick-or-treating is over Halloween night, most kids go home to the safety of their own homes. But many children living in orphanages and shelters don't have the comforting routines of bedtime to look forward to. **Genevieve Piturro** was volunteering to read to children at a homeless shelter when she learned that some kids had never even owned their own pair of pajamas. "They had no pajamas to change into," Genevieve recalls, "so I started to bring pajamas. One little girl stared at them and said, 'What are these?' From that moment on, I said I needed pajamas for these children." Genevieve wanted to help, so in 2001 she began the **Pajama Program** to make sure that every child living in such uncertainty gets the comfort of fresh pajamas and a good book to help them go to bed at night. "If everybody did one small thing, it would be an amazing change in the world," Genevieve says. Since the Pajama Program began, it has distributed nearly 500,000 pairs of pajamas to kids across the United States. "It's a small thing," she says, "but it's a big thing."

Learn more about the Pajama Program by visiting their website at www.PajamaProgram.org.

NOVEMBER

Please come to...
A FOOD-DRIVE PARTY!

What to bring:

The makings for Chili:
Canned red kidney beans
Canned tomato sauce

beans

Canned black beans
Canned diced tomatoes
Canned white beans
Chili seasoning packet
Canned corn

WHAT YOU CAN DO:

1. Host a canned-food drive at your school.
2. Bag up cans for a special recipe of vegetarian chili.
3. Make a Thanksgiving turkey from cookies.
4. Create a tin can turkey for your Thanksgiving table.
5. Check out Feeding America and how one little idea is feeding millions.

HOSTING A CANNED-FOOD DRIVE:

Collecting canned foods for the hungry in your community can go a long way toward helping families and individuals. Emphasize what healthy foods are needed, and watch your schoolmates chip in to help. Here are some suggestions of recommended items for your food drive:

Canned vegetables and fruits
Peanut butter
Canned tuna
Canned soups
Canned raviolis
Canned beef stews

CAN-DO SPIRIT!

When November rolls around, your thoughts may turn to Thanksgiving and good food. But many people in communities around the United States need help making ends meet. There are times when, once all the bills are paid, there's no money left over for groceries. That's where food pantries and soup kitchens come in, providing canned goods and warm meals to people who need it most. Try helping stock the shelves at your local food pantry by hosting a canned-food drive. And when you throw this party in the classroom, you can collect even more canned goods for the greater good!

Suggestions for a successful food drive:

- **Communicate:** Start with your classroom teacher. Make sure you have permission, and line up everything you'll need for a successful food drive. Contact your local food pantry to let them know your plans. Be sure to find out if they have any special needs.
- **Advertise:** Create your own flyers to hang up around your school in the two weeks leading up to the food drive. Print up enough so that teachers can send flyers home in their students' backpacks.
- **Work:** When the week of the food drive arrives, set up a table in the lobby of your school each morning before classes begin. Have members of your class work the table so they can take the bags from classmates each day, as well as inform other students about the project. They should be sure to thank everyone for participating, too!
- **Load:** Once the drive is over, contact the food pantry's Volunteer Coordinator to let them know you're coming with all the cans. You'll need classmates' parents to help drive the bags and boxes of canned goods over to the pantry.
- **Celebrate:** Once you've totaled up how many cans you delivered, create another food-drive flyer letting your schoolmates know how much they helped.

BAGGING UP CANS FOR VEGETARIAN CHILI:

November means colder temperatures. Try beating the chilly weather with some steaming hot chili! Ask your friends or classmates to supply the ingredients needed to make warm, nutritious chili. Then you can place those cans together in individual bags, write up the recipe on an index card, and tie it all up with a bright ribbon. It will make a great holiday treat that's healthy and hearty to eat.

Here's a simple recipe for vegetarian chili:

1 (15 ounce) can black beans
1 (15 ounce) can red kidney beans
1 (15 ounce) can white beans
1 (15 ounce) can corn
2 (14.5 ounce) cans diced tomatoes
1 (8 ounce) can tomato sauce
1 (1.25 ounce) Chili seasoning packet

Stir all ingredients together in a big pot and simmer uncovered for 30 minutes. Serves about 6.

MAKING A THANKSGIVING TURKEY FROM COOKIES:

You and your classmates can celebrate the season with a sweet snack. Try making a Thanksgiving turkey out of cookies for a gobbling good holiday treat.

Here's how:
• Take one cream-filled cookie like a Double Stuf Oreo brand cookie to use as the body of the turkey.

Poke about five candy corns into the creamy stuffing, all in a row. These are the turkey's tail feathers.

Take one Mini Oreo brand cookie and separate the sides, making sure to keep the cream together on one cookie (go ahead and eat the half that has no cream!).

Spread chocolate frosting or peanut butter over the blank side of the creamed cookie, and stick it onto the front of the larger Oreo cookie on the lower half of the cookie face. This will be the turkey's head.

MAKING A THANKSGIVING TURKEY FROM COOKIES:

Open a bag of candy like plain Mini M&Ms brand treats. Select two brown Mini M&Ms to use as eyes, and stick them into the white cream of the Mini Oreo cookie.

Nibble down the end of a candy corn until you have just an orange triangle. Stick this into the Mini Oreo cream to use as a beak. Point the triangle up and out.

Find a red Mini M&M to use as the turkey's wattle. Stick this just below the orange beak.

Sit back, admire your Thanksgiving turkey, and then gobble it down!

CREATING A TIN-CAN TURKEY TO TAKE HOME:

Decorate the Thanksgiving table at your house by creating a turkey centerpiece out of a tin can. Place flowers in the can to create a festive atmosphere, and let the tin can remind you of all the effort you put in to help your local food pantry.

Here's how to make it:

Clean and rinse one tin can. Be careful not to cut yourself on the sharp ridge.

Using brown construction paper, cut a strip to wrap completely around the can. Glue the seam down in back.

Cut out different colors of construction paper to make eight turkey feathers. Glue them along the back of the can.

Using white paper, cut out a scalloped circle to make the turkey's neck feathers. Glue it down on the front of the can just at the top lip. Fold down the top part of the scallops into the can.

Cut out a brown oval to make the turkey's head. Glue it onto the white scalloped feathers, being sure to leave a half inch of the head above the lip of the can.

Cut out two white ovals for eyes and glue them onto the head. Using black paper, cut out eyeballs and eyebrows, gluing them down onto the white circles and just above. Using yellow paper, cut out a triangle for your turkey's beak.

CREATING A TIN-CAN TURKEY TO TAKE HOME:

Make the turkey's wattle by cutting out two red ovals. Glue them down just below the turkey's head.

Using orange construction paper, cut out two feet shaped like triangles. Glue them to the bottom lip of the can front.

Use a water bottle or measuring cup with a lip, and gently fill your can with water. Make sure not to get the paper wet! Fill with chrysanthemums and other fall flowers, and enjoy!

ONE PERSON MAKING A DIFFERENCE:

John van Hengel once met a woman who had 10 children but couldn't feed them. She was digging through trash bins behind grocery stores looking for food that was old but still edible. John wanted to help her, so he began working on an idea. What if grocery stores and businesses donated old food that was still good but unwanted? He met with the mother again, and they talked about the need for a place that could accept all that old food — the way a bank accepts money. "When she said 'bank of food,' that rang a bell," John told the *Chicago Tribune* in 1988, "and we said: 'That's it. We'll call it a food bank.'" He decided to begin one, and in 1967, the nation's first food bank opened its doors. Originally called America's Second Harvest, his idea blossomed into a network of over 200 food banks serving people across the United States. "It's amazing how many people are being fed because of this crazy little thing we started," John told *The Los Angeles Times* in 1992. He died in 2005, but his simple idea — which is now known as **Feeding America** — feeds more than 25 million people each year.

For more information about Feeding America, check out their website at www.FeedingAmerica.org.

DECEMBER

Please come to...
A MITTENS, HATS AND SOCKS PARTY!

What to bring:
Winter gloves, mittens, hats, or socks
Skein of yarn

WHAT YOU CAN DO:

Throw a party in your classroom. Over two weeks, collect as many pairs of winter gloves, mittens, hats and warm socks as you can. Have your classmates hang them on a holiday tree as decorations. Then donate all your "ornaments" to a local organization that helps kids in need, and their families. Here's a quick list of party ideas:

1. **Decorate a holiday tree with mittens, hats and socks.**
2. **Knit scarves with your classmates to donate, too.**
3. **Make popcorn snowmen to eat in class.**
4. **Create sock snowmen to decorate your house.**
5. **Learn about Binky Patrol and sending warm, comforting blankets to kids in need.**

SPREAD THE WARMTH!

Wintertime means snowball fighting, fort building and making snow angels. It can be the most fun time of year if you have the right things to keep you warm. But many children who can't afford winter gear play in the snow with their bare hands. You can warm hearts and hands by throwing a party to collect mittens, hats and socks for families in your community. And by doing this activity in your classroom or school, you can get even more people involved to help. The more, the merrier!

DECORATING A TREE WITH MITTENS, HATS AND SOCKS:

Before you start, contact a local agency that works with families in need. Find out if they are collecting winter items for the people they help. Talk with the Volunteer Coordinator about when you can drop off your donations.

DECORATING A TREE WITH MITTENS, HATS AND SOCKS:

With your teacher's or principal's permission, set up a holiday tree in your classroom or the lobby of your school.

Over two weeks, have your classmates bring in warm winter items like wool hats, mittens, gloves and socks. Hang the items on the tree like holiday ornaments.

When the party is over, gather up all the winter gear and take it to the charity. And know that you won't just be warming hands, heads and feet, you'll be warming hearts as well.

KNITTING A SCARF WITH YOUR CLASSMATES:

Knitting is an age-old activity, dating back to the early Egyptians. It's been practiced by women and men for as long as people have been wearing clothes!

You and your classmates can learn to knit with just a few short lessons.

Contact a knitting or hobby shop and ask if they will lend your class a supply of knitting needles. Ask parents to send in theirs, too, until you have enough for everyone to participate.

Have everyone bring in a skein of yarn — enough for a single scarf.

Ask a teacher or parent to demonstrate a basic stitch.

Get knitting!

Along with all the hats, mittens and socks, donate your handmade scarf, as well. Be sure to attach a personal note letting the lucky recipient know that his or her new scarf was knitted with love.

MAKING POPCORN SNOWMEN:

Winter's bite doesn't have to be so bad when you have a fun treat to eat. Try sinking your teeth into an adorable popcorn snowman that you and your friends can make and devour yourselves.

12 cups popped popcorn
1 (10.5 ounce) package of marshmallows
4 tablespoons butter
1 teaspoon vanilla
Parchment paper
Candies for decoration

1. Melt the marshmallows and butter in the microwave. Remove from heat and stir in the vanilla. Set aside to cool for a few minutes. Then pour the mixture over the popped popcorn. Gently stir.

2. Rub your hands with butter to keep the popcorn from sticking. We recommend using one stick: half to go into the mixture, and the other half to rub on your hands. Keep it nearby, because this project gets messy! Form two popcorn balls with your hands – one slightly larger than the other. Place the balls on the parchment paper. Once they have set, stack the smaller ball on top of the larger.

3. Decorate the snowmen using candies. We recommend Skittles brand candy for eyes (save the orange ones to use as noses!). Large gumdrops are perfect for hats. Try red licorice, long taffy or Fruit by the Foot brand snacks to make a scarf.

Note: This recipe will make approximately 12 snowmen.

CREATING SOCK SNOWMEN TO TAKE HOME:

You can make a snowman decoration to brighten your house all winter long – and this snowman will never melt!

Here's what you'll need:
White tube socks (buy in bulk)
Pennies
Uncooked rice
White yarn
Buttons
Fabric scraps
Toothpicks
Glue gun

1. Take one men's tube sock and pour about 10 to 20 pennies into the toe. This will help the snowman keep balanced.

2. Pour in a cup of uncooked rice. Twist the sock, then tie it off with white yarn. This is the first ball of the snowman.

3. Pour in a little less of the uncooked rice to make the second ball. Twist the sock, then tie it off with white yarn.

4. Pour in the rice to make the third and smallest ball. This is the snowman's head.

5. Twist the sock and tie it off with white yarn. There should be enough sock left to fold over to make the top hat.

6. Using a hot glue gun (and a grownup's help), affix two buttons for eyes and a button in the center of the middle ball. Choose a red or other bright button for a mouth.

CREATING SOCK SNOWMEN TO TAKE HOME:

7. Using scrap fabric, cut out a long strip to make a scarf to tie around the snowman's neck. Using red felt, glue material around the top for his hat.

8. Glue a button or piece of holly on top of this to give the hat pizzazz.

9. Dip a toothpick in orange paint and poke into the snowman's head to make the carrot nose.

ONE PERSON MAKING A DIFFERENCE:

Mittens and socks aren't the only thing to keep you warm during the winter months. A soft, snuggly blanket can do wonders for body and soul. That's what **Susan Finch** thought when she started **Binky Patrol** back in 1996. Susan wanted to reach out to the "invisible kids," children suffering through traumatic events in shelters and foster homes, who are often forgotten by the rest of society. "When kids are scared, they need a reminder that somebody cares about them," Susan says. She estimates that Binky Patrol volunteers have sewn, knit, crocheted and quilted more than 500,000 comforting binky blankets for children around the United States. How does the group work? Kids and grownups alike can make small homemade blankets on their own or in groups to distribute wherever they see children in need. Binky Patrol mails out labels to be sewn into the corner of the blankets before they're handed out. Susan's goal was to keep the organization simple, without a lot of rules: "Just make it soft, washable and purely from your heart, and that's it. Just watch for pins." What does she tell kids who want to do something to help their communities? "When the opportunity is there," Susan advises, "just say yes. Go for it!"

Check out Binky Patrol's website at www.BinkyPatrol.org

TIPS FOR PARENTS AND TEACHERS

Be enthusiastic: One of the most important factors in children's philanthropic development is having the support of adults in their lives. If your child or class has expressed an interest in hosting a party, they'll need your enthusiastic support.

Be realistic: As with any celebration or gathering, there are costs involved. Look over the activities presented here and modify them to fit your budget. Take ideas from any of the months and tailor them to suit you.

Be smart: Plan in advance – while being spontaneous is fun, you can cut costs by collecting some items over time or picking up supplies when they are on sale. You'll note there are several activities listed that require items that you might already have at home: an old pillowcase, shoe box, milk carton, used sports equipment and several of the ingredients for the recipes. Purchase items in bulk wherever possible. Craft supplies can often be purchased in multiples through local craft stores or online.

Be a role model: If you are a parent, chances are that your kids know about your efforts to help others. But students might not be aware of their teachers' outside activities. Take a moment to tell your class about any volunteering you do – they'll be excited to learn more about your favorite charities.

Be positive: Offer positive feedback to encourage young children to participate. If your class hosts a party at school, make sure other members of the school community know about it. Give your class a chance to share what they learned and what they accomplished with the school, through announcements, bulletins or assemblies.

Be organized: Parties can involve a lot of planning. Involve your child in the organization of the party. The goal of these events is to empower children, which means they should be involved in as much of the work as possible. Have them make invitations and write out lists of supplies needed. Recruit another parent to help out, or in the classroom, put those room parents to work! Make sure you prepare as much in advance as you can, so that the party runs smoothly. And don't forget to have the kids help clean up afterward. It all contributes to their sense of accomplishment.

Be generous: With each month, we have put the spotlight on an individual or couple who started out with an idea for helping others and turned it into something much bigger. If one of these groups – or any other charity – appeals to your child, encourage your child to donate to that group. Some of the activities we suggest will generate funds: the lemonade stand, bake sales. Making a monetary donation to a favorite organization can be powerful for children. Even just a small amount will let them feel they are making a difference and further encourage their participation in philanthropic ventures.

FUNDRAISING IDEAS

ere are four simple ideas for raising money for charities:

Sell a product: bake sales, lemonade stands, craft rojects.

2. Solicit donations: ask for donations or pledges for a cause.

3. Perform a service: hold a car wash, help a neighbor, walk a dog.

4. Host an event: throw a party where you can do any or all of the above.

The Good Fun! Book

Final note:

The recipes and projects presented in this book have been happy collaborations between the authors, who extend their deepest gratitude to the beleaguered members of their families for their roles as cooking and crafting guinea pigs.

The projects presented here are meant to create a little fun while achieving a simple goal: teaching kids that they are part of something bigger than themselves. The entire effort has been a labor of love with the sole intention of engaging kids socially, with each other and with the communities where they live; intellectually, by getting them to think about big issues such as hunger, poverty and illiteracy; and emotionally, through the feelings that community service can engender.

The authors hope you enjoy it all, both the good and the fun!

BIOGRAPHIES:

Karen Duncan:

Karen Duncan made backyard bird houses and homemade ice cream when she was growing up in Tasmania. A former school teacher and athletic director at the University of Chicago Laboratory Schools, Karen follows education issues closely as the wife of U.S. Secretary of Education Arne Duncan. She lives in Virginia with her husband and two children, a cat, and lots of sports equipment.

Kate Hannigan Issa:

Kate Hannigan Issa helped sew groovy blue-jeans bags with her mom when she was growing up in Oklahoma. A professional editor and writer, Kate works on children's fiction and nonfiction when she isn't holding lemonade stands with her three children and husband in Chicago.

Anthony LeTourneau

Anthony LeTourneau drew every moment possible growing up. Even now he draws or paints every day and spends his free time learning and reading about being creative. Anthony (or as his friends call him, "Tony") was raised in the suburbs of St. Paul, Minnesota, and later moved with his wife and three boys to the Minnesota north woods, where he resides today.

NOTES: